A stitch in time...

A stitch in time...

**Life's
most
essential
hand-sewn
repairs**

Stewart, Tabori & Chang · New York

Published by
Stewart, Tabori & Chang
A Company of La Martinière Groupe
115 West 18th Street
New York, NY 10011

Export Sales to all countries except Canada, France,
and French-speaking Switzerland:
Thames and Hudson Ltd.
181A High Holborn
London WC1V 7QX
England

Canadian Distribution:
Canadian Manda Group
One Atlantic Avenue, Suite 105
Toronto, Ontario M6K 3E7
Canada

Library of Congress Cataloging-in-Publication Data

Taylor, Clarice.
        A stitch in time : life's most essential sewing-machine-less repairs / by Clarice Taylor.
           p. cm.
        ISBN 1-58479-324-4
        1. Clothing and dress–Repairing. 2. Sewing. I. Title.

TT720.T39 2004
646'.6–dc22

                                                                2003066803

Printed in China

10 9 8 7 6 5 4 3 2 1

First Printing

To the female elders of my blood—Millers, Weathers, Spencers, and Steeles—but most of all to my mother Edna Miller Taylor

A stitch in time... would not have been possible without help at the very beginning from Gilbert Fletcher and initial encouragement from Ruth Kogan to develop the idea. Toni Barton and Susan Oliver were like blessed angels sent from heaven, with divine photography and sewing skills, respectively. The team at STC—starting with the visionary Marisa Bulzone and wonderfully supportive Leslie Stoker and ending with the creative Larissa Nowicki and conscientious Elaine Schiebel—gave this simple idea brilliant form. Thank you all.

Introduction

Imagine a scenario: at the center of the action is the elder, demonstrating excellence, passing on techniques perfected over the years, lacing the practical instruction with proverbs for living. The message is self-reliance in the homely arts.

The scene changes to our time and culture. Today, being able to work with one's hands still means freedom.

The basic skills in this book are important to learn or have at one's fingertips, if only to reclaim favorite possessions from the "to be donated" pile. After all, that's your favorite shirt. It still looks great on you, and when you wear it you feel you can conquer the world. You need that feeling as you prepare to take your final exams. If only you hadn't torn the buttonhole. And your monthly allowance from home doesn't allow for the expense of taking it to a tailor.

Or perhaps you've taken the red-eye to attend an important business meeting in another city. You arrive at the hotel with time enough and a little to spare. You've showered and reviewed your notes over breakfast, but find while dressing that the hem of your suit jacket is hanging down. You have to leave in fifteen minutes if you're going to be on time. But it will take at least forty minutes for the hotel valet to collect, repair, and return it.

Maybe you own a dress that earns you the most extravagant compliments. It brings out the color of your eyes and the grace of your form. It cost a lot but was worth every penny. No wonder you rushed to the dry cleaner to have the zipper replaced when it broke. What a shock when you are ready to wear it again and notice that the new zipper has been sewn in with not-quite-matching thread!

Working with your own hands can mean freedom from dependence on the dry cleaner or tailor. It can mean an end to frustration at less-than-excellent-quality work and exorbitant cost. It can extend the life of your favorite items and save valuable time.

Working with your hands can also bring fulfillment and accomplishment. Using traditional home arts in their purely practical applications, simplifies our complex lives.

This little book teaches basic techniques of sewing-machineless sewing, the most basic home art, not in the abstract, but for use in today's busy lives. It also beautifully presents the key techniques for hand-sewing, honoring the simple traditions from which these needle arts are drawn and preserving them for the future. It echoes the voice of the elder many of us never had. If you didn't have the chance to sit with Grandma as she darned the holes in a pair of socks that had a good deal of wear left in them, or to observe the fabric artist of your clan as she stitched together the pieces of a quilt that is now a family heirloom, **A stitch in time...** is for you.

Business men and women on the road, newlyweds and new parents, as well as the collegebound will all discover that this little book will equip them to make repairs in the nick of time—saving more effort and cost later on. *A stitch in time...* includes thirteen of the basic, must-know stitches for absolute beginners and is seasoned with the wisdom and love of the elders from many places and times.

Your Basic Sewing Box

Fill your sewing box with quality tools and equipment

Quality is worth the investment. Once you've bought the best you can afford, remember to maintain your sewing tools with your own version of a 10,000 mile checkup. You will find that good tools make your sewing tasks easier and ensure better results. There are many more tools on the market than are needed for the purposes of this book. No gadgets here. These are the basics, the equipment you should have on hand for time-, money-, and clothes-saving emergency repairs.

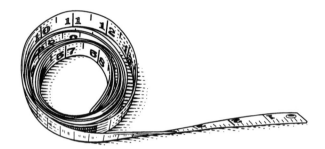

Measuring

Tape Measure The most useful tape measure is at least 60 inches long with metal tabs on each end. Check to see that measurements are marked clearly on both sides, starting at opposite ends, preferably in both inches and centimeters. Also, be sure it is made of a material that does not stretch.

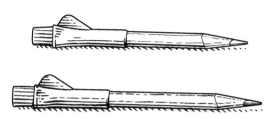

Marking

Tailor's chalk For marking placements for such things as buttons and lost hooks, or tracking alterations, clay chalk is ideal. It lasts while you are sewing and can be removed easily when the garment is cleaned or laundered. It comes in pencil form or in squares and is available in a variety of colors.

Cutting

Scissors Good quality scissors and shears will last a lifetime. Use them only to cut fabric and keep another pair on hand for household chores and heavy paper or cardboard. Keeping your scissors sharp is essential to prolonging their life. See if your local hardware store or sewing machine repair shop provides this service.

Sewing and embroidery scissors These scissors have two sharp points, making them ideal for cutting buttonholes, clipping seams, and other work that requires accuracy. I've found them to be most useful in 4-inch or 5-inch lengths.

Dressmaker's shears Specifically for cutting fabric, these shears have bent handles that allow fabric to lie flat as you cut. You probably won't use them often for emergency repairs, but they will come in handy in making patches and you might find that you love sewing and move on to quilting or actually making garments. If you decide to include these shears in your sewing box, choose a pair that is 7 or 8 inches long. Models for lefties are available.

sewing scissors

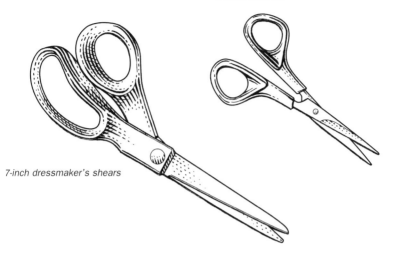

7-inch dressmaker's shears

embroidery scissors

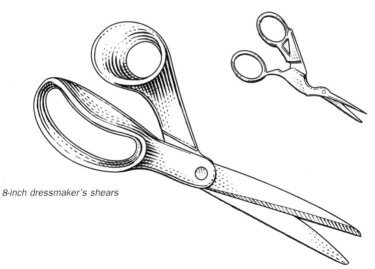

8-inch dressmaker's shears

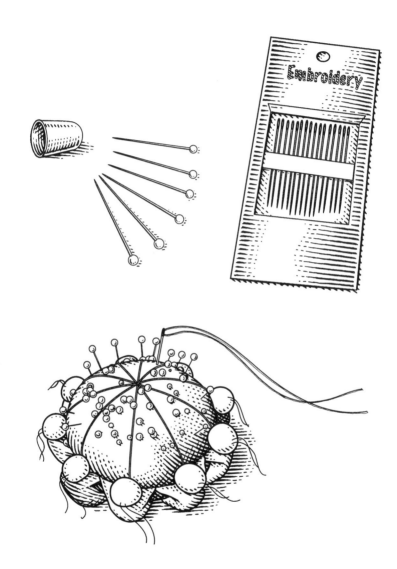

Sewing

Needles Buy quality brands. Off brands can dull and rust easily. Ask the staff where you buy your sewing supplies for their top brands. Keep a variety of needle sizes and types on hand. I especially appreciate self-threading needles; they save time and frustration.

Straight pins For general use, buy quality brand size 17 rustproof pins. They are available with plain or plastic heads and come in extra thin, extra long, and in magnetic wire. Magnetic pins are available but they tend to stick together and to metal surfaces, and can be more trouble than they are worth.

Pincushion There is nothing like it to keep your sewing surface neat and avoid losing pins. Many different kinds are available, including magnetic pincushions for use with steel pins. For ease of movement, a wrist pincushion can be very handy. You can buy them ready-made or make one easily by sewing a pincushion to a bracelet of elastic.

Thimble Essential for hand-sewing, a thimble protects your thumb or fingers from the needle, helping you complete your projects faster and easier and with more professional results. They come in metal and plastic and should fit the middle finger of your sewing hand.

Thread Available in a wide range of colors, weights, and fibers, choose thread based on the fabric you are sewing and the type of repair.

Seam ripper A handy tool for removing thread without damaging fabric.

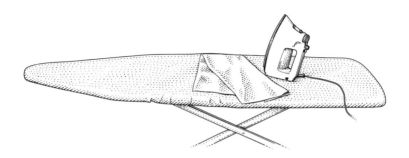

Pressing

Iron Pressing is the final step in most sewing repairs, as it fixes the shape or edge. Invest in a good iron with an accurate temperature gauge. An iron with steam and dry functions is a must.

Ironing Board Be sure your ironing board is firm, well-padded, and adjustable in height. A removable cover is essential for keeping it clean.

Press Cloth Unbleached muslin, thoroughly washed, or cheesecloth with a close weave are as effective as commercially prepared press cloths. A woolen cloth can give good results when working with woolen garments.

General Tips for Making Quick Repairs

Train your head and hands to do,
your head and heart to dare.

JOSEPH SEAMON COTTER, JR.

It's easy to make repairs when you know how, and these tips will help take the sting out of sewing and turn the experience into a pleasure.

- Always work in good light. It seems obvious, but you'd be surprised at the difference light can make.

- Make sure you have plenty of room. Clear space on a table or have on hand a folding cutting board that can be used on a bed or to enlarge a small tabletop.

- Choose good-quality materials and tools, especially when it comes to thread. Buy name brands; cheap thread is likely to break and shred.

- Use matching thread even where it doesn't show. This reflects an attitude of doing quality work in every area of life.

- Keep thread in standard colors on hand—black, white, cream, brown, navy blue, gray, and red.

- Keep a hotel-type mini sewing kit in your briefcase or purse.

- With the exception of sewing on buttons, hand-sewing is done with a single thread.

- Cut thread at an angle. It makes threading the needle easier.

- Hand stitches should be very close together, 12 or more stitches to the inch.

- Hand-sewing is done from right to left, unless otherwise noted.

The Seven Essential Stitches for Quick Repairs

Begin and end right

How you begin and end a stitch will determine its strength. Finish a seam by making a tiny backstitch catching a single thread of fabric and leaving a small loop in the thread. Then make another backstitch, running the needle through the loop in the thread. Pull tight. Repeat for greater strength. A triple backstitch—three stitches one on top of the other—is a good choice instead of a knot, especially if you are working with light or delicate fabrics.

1

Even Backstitch

The even backstitch is the strongest and most durable hand stitch. It can look like machine stitching and is great for seams and hard working areas like elbows, knees and seats.

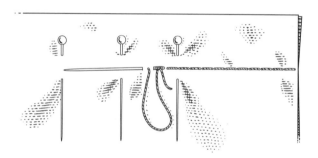

1. Start by pulling your needle up through the fabric at the stitching line.

2. Poke the needle back into the fabric about $1/16$ of an inch to the right.

3. Slip the needle under the fabric, bringing it up $1/8$ inch to the left.

4. Poke the needle in the fabric at the beginning of the first stitch, making another stitch $1/16$ inch long.

5. Repeat steps 4 through 7 moving backward and forward, making a continuous row of stitching. Stitch $1/2$ inch over original, unbroken stitches at the end and knot the thread.

2

Buttonhole Stitch

This stitch has a special loop that makes a stable edge and clean finish. Use matching Buttonhole Twist, a strong silk thread ideal for hand-sewn buttons and button holes.

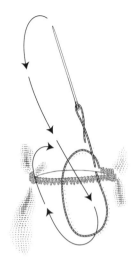

1. Poke the needle in the fabric from the wrong side... from the wrong side about $^1/_{16}$ inch from the cut edge of the buttonhole.

2. Hold the two threads near the eye of the needle and slip them under the needle from right to left.

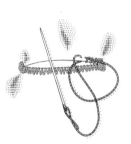

3. Pull the needle through to form an extra loop.

4. As you pull the thread away firmly but not too tightly, the loop will fall exactly on the edge of the buttonhole opening.

5. Make the second stitch by poking the needle from the wrong side close to the first stitch. Make sure to stitch through the fabric and the patch.

6. Repeat steps 2 through 5 on either side of buttonhole to its end.

3

Hemming Stitch

This stitch is used to hold a folded edge in place.

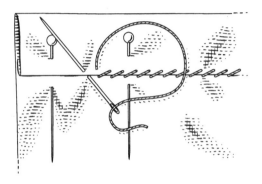

1. Working from the inside of the garment, fasten the thread to the hem allowance (the part that's folded against the inside of the garment) by poking the needle through the fold of the hem's top edge and bringing it up through the fabric about $1/4$ to $1/8$ of an inch from where it entered.
2. With the point of the needle, pick up one or two threads from the garment fabric and work the needle back into the fold of the hem's top edge.
3. Poke the needle back through the fold of the hem edge and bring it up through the fabric.

4

Running Stitch

This is a tiny, even stitch used for mending, gathering, shirring, and quilting. It is one of the easiest to do.

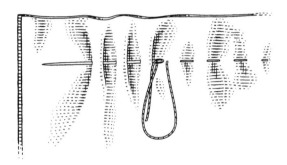

1. Working on the wrong side of the garment, pick up a small amount of fabric with the needle.
2. Work the needle in and out of the fabric in a weaving motion until there are several stitches gathered on it.
3. Pull the needle though the material and secure or, if you are repairing or patching a hole, start a new series of running stitches until you have several rows of close stitching across the patch.

5

Sloating Stitch

This is the ideal stitch to repair rips or cuts in heavy fabric.

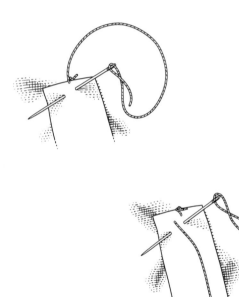

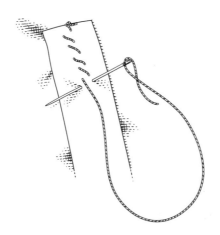

1. Using thread that closely matches your garment, take a stitch $\frac{1}{2}$ inch before the tear, picking up two or three threads only on the right side of the garment so that it doesn't show.

2. Poke the needle through about $\frac{1}{16}$ inch from the edge of the tear. Work it through the fabric coming out about $\frac{1}{16}$ inch from the tear on the opposite side.

3. Make the next stitch about $\frac{1}{16}$ inch from the first—again, never piercing the right side of the fabric but picking up only a few threads.

4. Repeat steps 2 and 3 stitching $\frac{1}{2}$ inch past the end of the tear and back-stitch. The repair should be invisible on the right side of the garment but appear as a small slanting stitch on the wrong side.

6

Slipstitch

This stitch can be used to temporarily hold seams or two pieces of fabric together before using a permanent stitching technique.

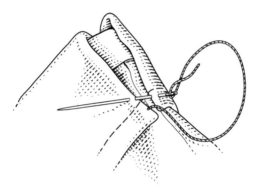

1. Make a stitch on the seam line of the lower edge.
2. Slip the needle into the upper section in the seam line fold, bringing the needle out again on the fold line about $1/4$ inch away.
3. Poke the needle in the lower seam line directly below the point from which it just emerged.

7

Pick Stitch

This stitch works well for hand-sewing or reattaching a zipper.

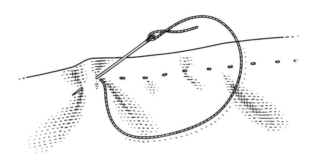

1. With the needle through the garment on the right side, pick up one or two threads.
2. Push the needle through the fabric on the diagonal, emerging $^1/_4$ inch to the left.
3. Continue for the length of the seam pulling each stitch tight.

Quick repairs—A baker's dozen

The following basic repairs are important to have at your fingertips

They need not be "memorized." Simply follow along step by step, applying the instructions to your project. Remember to read each through carefully before you begin. Sometimes a bit of improvisation will be necessary, but that's what makes even these simplest sewing skills an art.

1

Hem Repair

The slipstitch is excellent for repairing a hem. The stitch is very durable and almost invisible.

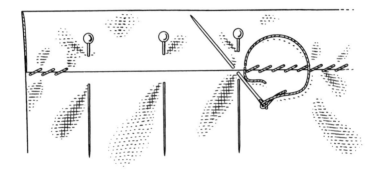

1. Begin by pinning the fallen hem into place with straight pins at right angles to the hem allowance. Place the pins close enough together to keep the hem allowance flat against the inside of the garment.

2. Thread your needle with a single strand of thread no longer than about 18 to 25 inches to avoid tangling.

3. Working from the inside of the garment, poke the needle through the hem's top edge (the fold) and bring it up through the fabric about $1/4$ to $1/8$ of an inch to the left—unless you are a lefty, in which case you may be more comfortable sewing from left to right.

4. Using the point of the needle, pick up one or two threads of the garment fabric, then poke the needle back into the fold of the hem's top edge.

5. Poke the needle back through the fold of the hem edge and bring it up through the fabric, again, picking up only one or two threads so the stitch is virtually invisible on the outside.

6. Repeat steps 3 and 4, making sure your stitches are firm but loose enough for a little give, until the hem is reattached.

7. Secure your new hem by making a small backstitch to the right and forming a loop over the point of the needle.

8. Pull the thread through the loop to cinch the thread and place the knot flat against the fabric. For extra security, sew two knots for pants hems or other hard-working areas.

2

Sew on a Button

This method can be also be used to secure dangling buttons. It takes only minutes and is the same for sew-through buttons with two or four holes. Excavate for that extra button that came with the brand new garment. If you've misplaced it, check an inside seam, as manufacturers sometimes affix extras there. Another solution is to reappropriate one of the buttons from the cuff. If you do, remove its mate, for symmetry's sake, from the other sleeve. (Tuck it away with your sewing arsenal for the next time.)

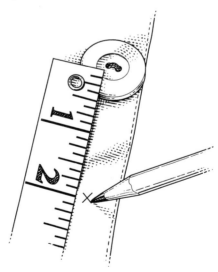

1. Usually, a lost button leaves tiny holes in the fabric, showing the correct placement. If not, line up the button hole and use dressmaker's chalk to mark the spot on the garment where the button is to go.

2. Sewing on a button is the one hand-sewing technique that calls for a double rather than single strand of thread. Make it about 18 inches long and knot each strand separately to avoid tangling.

3. Starting on the wrong side of the fabric, poke the needle through the fabric so that the knot is on the mark.

4. Create a tack to place the button by bringing the needle back through the fabric not more than $1/8$ inch away from the mark.

5. Poke the needle through one of the holes of the button.

6. Create a shank or spacer between the fabric and the button so it can go smoothly through the buttonhole. Place a toothpick or matchpoke on top of the button between the holes.

7. Poke the needle down through the hole opposite to the one you started with and pull the thread tight.

8. Continue by poking the needle back and forth between the holes of the button at least twice for each set of holes.

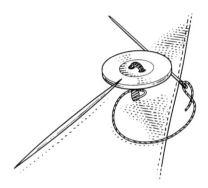

9. Once you've secured the button to the fabric, remove the toothpick.

10. To finish, poke the needle through one of the holes in the button and then through the fabric so that the needle comes out between the button and the fabric.

11. Wrap the thread tightly around the threads between the button and the fabric three times to secure the shank.

12. Tie a knot by pushing the needle through a loop of thread as it goes around the shank, pulling the thread tight to make a knot.

13. Clip thread close to the shank.

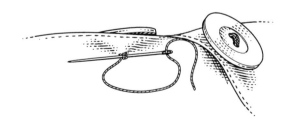

3

Darn a Hole

1. Start with lightweight darning thread that closely matches your garment. If you can't find your color or you are in a pinch, all-purpose thread will do.

2. Thread a long darning needle using a short, double strand. Start without a knot, but leave a bit of thread end on the wrong side of the garment.

3. Working on the wrong side of the garment, strengthen the raw or frayed edge of the hole by making neat, tiny running stitches around the edge of the hole.

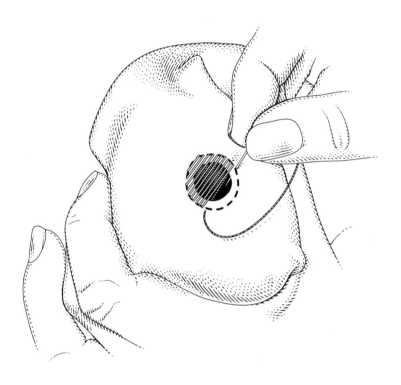

4. With the hole at its center, place the garment over a hard, round surface to slightly stretch and support the fabric. Sew close, parallel rows of long, flat running stitches back and forth across the hole to cover the entire area.

5. Weave thread in and out of running stitches at right angles to fill them in, picking up tiny threads of the garment fabric as you go.

6. Pull thread to the wrong side of the garment and clip end when finished.

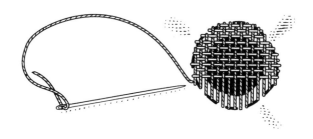

4

Repair a Ripped Seam

This technique applies to simple ripped seams where the thread is broken and the fabric is not ripped.

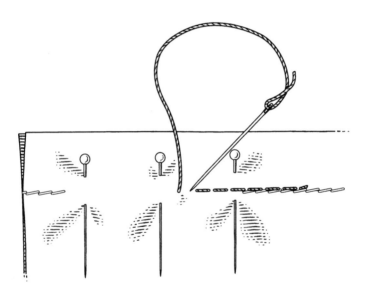

1. Turn the garment inside out and remove the broken thread by trimming it close to the seam or removing it with a seam ripper or pin.

2. Pin the seam allowances back together, edge to edge, to hold them in place as you sew.

3. Start your line of new stitches about a $1/2$ inch over the intact seam to reinforce the joining. Use a back-stitch to hold it securely.

4. Using the even backstitch—the strongest and most durable hand stitch—pull the needle up through the fabric at the stitching line.

5. Poke the needle back into the fabric about $1/16$ of an inch to the right.

6. Slip the needle under the fabric, bringing it up $1/8$ inch to the left.

7. Poke the needle in the fabric at the beginning of the first stitch, making another stitch $1/16$ inch long.

8. Repeat steps 4 through 7 moving backward and forward, making a continuous row of stitching. Be sure to make your new stitches $1/2$ inch over the old, unbroken stitches on the other side of the tear and knot the thread.

5

Repair a Tear in a Garment

Grandma would have accomplished many such repairs using only a sloating stitch. However, since we have the technology, why not add extra strength with fusible interfacing? Cut a piece that is $\frac{1}{2}$-inch wide and the length of the tear, plus 1 inch for extra reinforcement.

1. Trim off the loose or frayed ends of the tear.
2. Lay the garment on the ironing board and bring the raw edges of the tear as close together as possible. Using a warm iron (check manufacturer's instructions) fuse the interfacing to the tear on the wrong side of the garment. Let it cool.

3. Using thread that closely matches your garment make a stitch $1/2$ inch before the tear, picking up two or three threads only on the right side of the garment so that it doesn't show.

4. Poke the needle through about $1/16$ inch from the edge of the tear. Work it through the fabric coming out about $1/16$ inch from the tear on the opposite side.

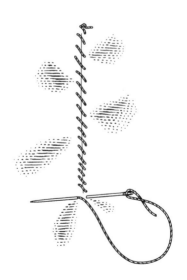

5. Make the next stitch about $^1/_{16}$ inch from the first, picking up only a few threads and never completely piercing the right side of the fabric.

6. Repeat steps 3 through 5 stitching $^1/_2$ inch past the end of the tear. Back-stitch. The repair should be invisible on the right side of the garment but appear as a small slanting stitch on the wrong side.

7. If the tear is in an area that gets heavy wear such as elbows, knees or seat, you might want to make a second line of stitching to crisscross—a kind of hand-sewn zigzag.

6

Mend a Tear Under a Button

1. If your lost button left a hole behind, it is a good idea to reinforce it before replacing the button. Matching iron-on mending tape cut in a circle or oval fused to the wrong side of the garment works well.

2. If you don't have an iron or tape, it is easy to make a patch. Cut out a circular piece of closely matching fabric of a circumference $1/4$ to $1/2$ inch larger than the hole.

3. Pin the patch in place to the wrong side of the garment, centering the patch under the hole.

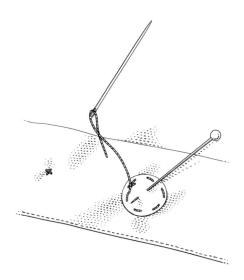

4. Use small slip stitches to secure the patch to your garment.
5. Continuing to work on the wrong side of the fabric, pick up a small amount of fabric with the needle.
6. Use the running stitch, poking the needle in and out of the fabric and the patch in a weaving motion until several stitches are gathered on it.

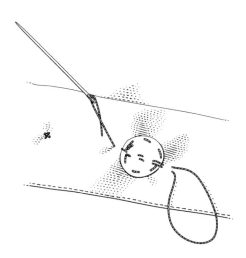

7. Pull the needle though the material making sure the stitches extend just beyond the patch.

8. Repeat steps 6 and 7 until you have several rows of close stitching across the patch.

9. Replace the button (see page 38).

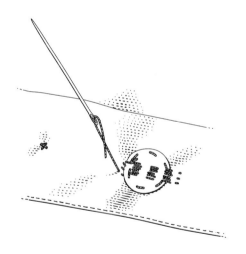

7

Repair a Button Hole

1. Trim away any loose threads or frayed ends from the buttonhole.

2. Reinforce the worn or torn area by ironing on a small fusible patch in a matching color. If you don't have an iron-on patch handy, you can hand-sew a small piece of matching fabric (see Mend a Tear Under a Button, steps 2–3).

3. Thread your needle with heavyweight matching thread no longer than 18 inches long.

4. Working from right to left, secure the thread so the ends will be invisible by poking the needle into the fabric and through the patch from the wrong side about $1/16$ inch from the cut edge of the button hole.

5. Hold the two threads near the eye of the needle and slip them under the needle from right to left.

6. Pull the needle through to form an extra loop.

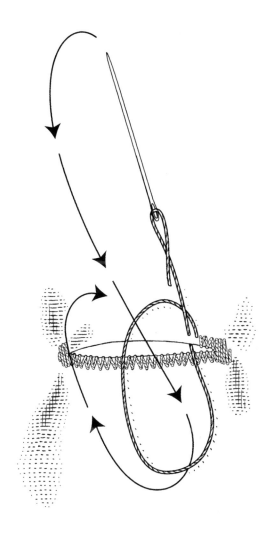

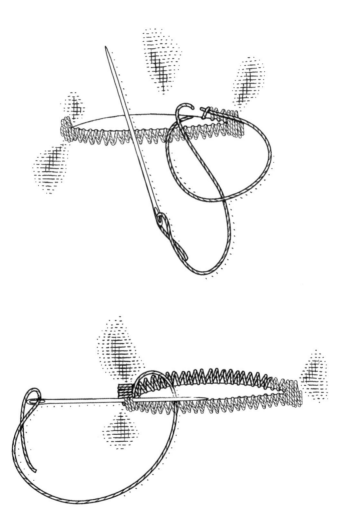

7. As you pull the thread away firmly but not too tightly, the loop will fall exactly on the edge of the buttonhole.

8. Make the second stitch by poking the needle from the wrong side of the fabric close to the first stitch. Be sure to stitch through both the fabric and the patch.

9. Repeat steps 5 through 8 on either side of buttonhole to its end.

10. Restitch the end of the buttonhole across the opening, overlapping the old stitching with the new.

11. Use small, sharp scissors to recut the buttonhole opening.

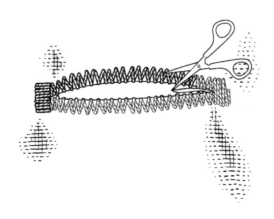

8

Replace Elastic

This repair works well for elastic that is held in a casing but not sewn directly to the garment.

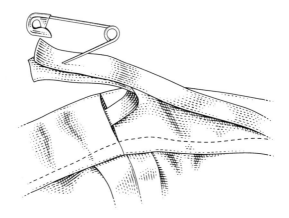

1. Cut a new piece of elastic the same width as the old, being careful to add an extra 1 inch for the seam.
2. Use sharp scissors to make a small opening in the seam on the wrong side of the casing.
3. Cut old elastic and join new elastic to it with a safety pin.
4. Pull old elastic, drawing new piece into the casing except the last 2 inches.
5. Keep a secure hold on the end of the new piece and unpin the old elastic from the new, making sure it is lying flat in the casing.

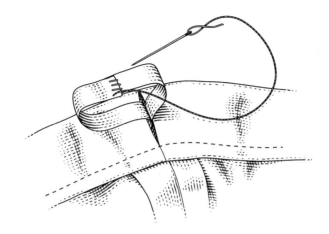

6. Overlap both ends of the new piece and join them by taking diagonal stitches (all in the same direction) over the raw edge.

7. Keep the stitches $\frac{1}{8}$ to $\frac{1}{4}$ inch deep and evenly spaced at about $\frac{1}{2}$ inch apart.

8. Slipstitch to close up seam as follows, re-aligning original seam allowances one edge folded under the other, and pinning in position.

9. Make a stitch on the seam line of the lower edge.

10. Slip the needle into the upper section in the seam line fold, bringing the needle out again on the fold line about $\frac{1}{4}$ inch away.

11. Poke the needle in the lower seam line directly below the point from which it just emerged.

12. Follow steps 9 through 11 until seam is closed, then use the back stitch and knot.

9

Replace a Broken Zipper

Hand-sewing a zipper is a useful emergency repair and generally a stop gap until you can get to a sewing machine or tailor. If you are working on pants or a skirt and there is a waistband, rip it back just enough to remove the old zipper. You might want to make notes on how the zipper was installed to help you put it back together: otherwise, the method below works well to replace a set-in zipper.

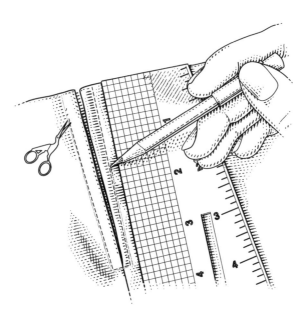

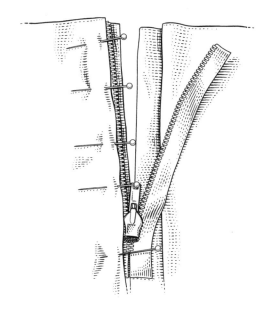

1. Use a replacement zipper the same length as the zipper opening.

2. Mark the original topstitching line with dressmaker's chalk or tape.

3. Unzip and carefully rip out the stitching that attaches the broken zipper to the garment using a small, sharp pair of scissors or a seam ripper.

4. Unzip and separate the two sides of the replacement zipper.

5. If the garment is lined, open it so that it lies flat.

6. Using dressmaker's or straight pins, pin one side of the zipper to the lining with right sides together so that the zipper pull faces the outside of the garment.

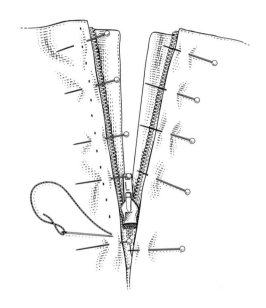

7. Using the pick stitch, sew the first side of the zipper through one layer of the lining, stitching down the center of the zipper tape.

8. Working on the right side of the garment, pin the opening over the first side of the zipper, pinning through all the layers of fabric.

9. Again, use the pick stitch to topstitch over the original topstitching line: Working from right to left, start by poking the needle through to the right side of the fabric and make a small, neat stitch.

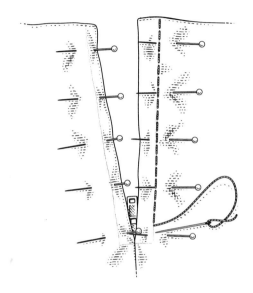

10. Poke the needle at the end of the previous stitch making another stitch $1/16$ inch long.

11. Repeat steps 9 and 10, moving backward and then forward, making a continuous row of stitches that looks like machine stitching.

10

Replace a Lost Hook and Eye

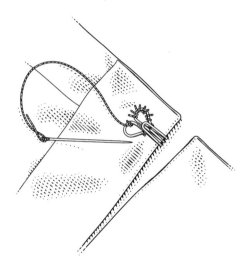

1. Working on the inside of the garment, make two stitches over the neck of the hook to secure it.
2. Stitch around each hole of the hook, picking up only one or two threads of fabric so the stitches do not show on the outside of the garment.
3. Place the eye so that the loop extends $1/8$ inch from the fabric edge.
4. Stitch over each side of the eye, fastening it securely to the garment.

5. Stitch each hole of the eye to the fabric, again, being careful not to let the stitches show on the outside of the garment.

6. Fasten the hook to the eye ensuring that neither can be seen on the outside of the garment.

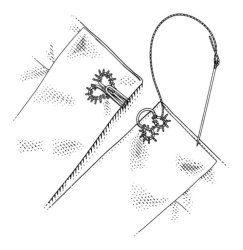

11

Replace Snap Fasteners

1. Using medium weight cotton or polyester thread in a color that matches your garment, poke the needle through the fabric to fasten the thread firmly to the wrong side of the overlapping edge.

2. Stitch the ball stud to this edge, four stitches through each hole, without stitching through to the right side.

3. Backstitch at the base.

4. Snap the ball stud and socket stud together.

5. Poke a pin through the center of the ball stud to the underlapping edge and mark with another pin for placement of the socket stud.

6. As with the ball stud, stitch the socket stud firmly to the underlapping edge using four stitches for each hole and backstitching at the base.

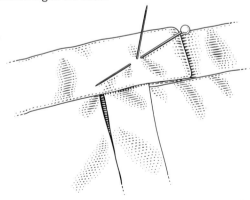

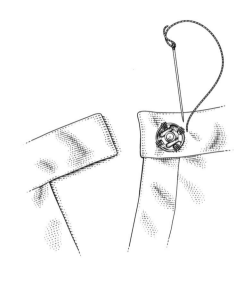

12

Mend a Torn Pocket

Here are quick repairs for both inseam and patch pockets.

Patch Pockets

1. Remove broken thread with a seam ripper or pin.

2. With your iron on the appropriate setting, press the pocket's seam allowance under to lie flat at the seam line.

3. Using dressmaker's or straight pins, pin the pocket back into place.

4. Thread your needle with a medium weight cotton or polyester thread in a color that matches the garment. If the garment features contrasting top stitching, match that.

5. Use the backstitch to reattach the pocket, overlapping $1/4$ inch on the still intact stitches at the beginning and end.

6. Knot the thread on the inside of the garment.

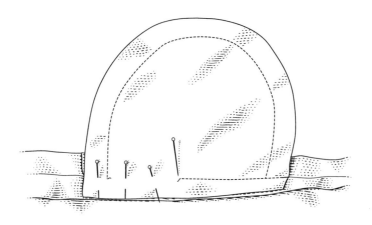

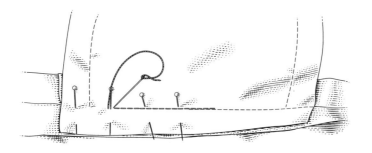

In-Seam Pockets Set into the seams of pants, skirts and coats, torn in-seam pockets are the cause of lost change and missing keys. Here is a quick repair that can be done in minutes.

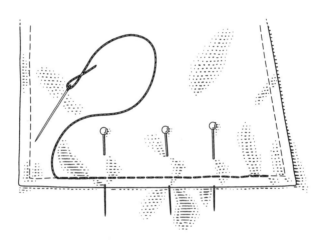

1. Remove broken thread.
2. Pin separated edges together with straight pins.
3. Using the backstitch, sew edges together along seam allowance, overlapping intact stitching on both ends.
4. Press seam open.

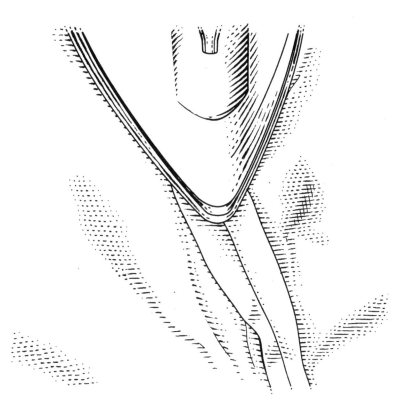

13

Close a Splayed Dart

Since this repair is done on the inside of a garment, the color of the thread is not critical, but, it is always more pleasing to do repairs with an eye toward quality. Use matching thread anyway, in a weight that is appropriate for the garment.

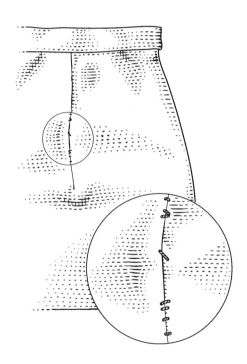

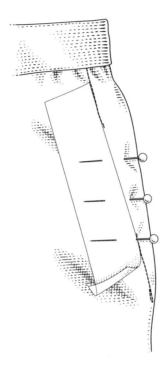

1. Working on the inside of the garment, pin the splayed dart right sides together along the fold line.

2. Press sides together.

3. Place a strip of invisible tape next to the stitching line for the length of the dart. The tape serves as a template for a straight sewing line.

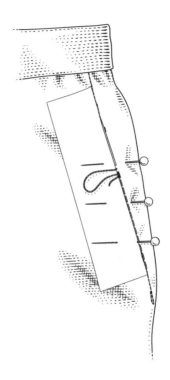

4. Starting at the widest end of the dart, overlapping $1/2$ inch with the still intact stitches, use the backstitch along the edge of the tape to replace the broken stitching.

5. Back-tack at the end and press the dart flat against garment.

Sources

National and Online Sewing Supply Retailers

Fabric.com

Online retailer of fabrics and sewing supplies.

2151 Northwest Parkway

Suite 500

Marietta, GA 30067

Tel: 888 455-2940

www.fabric.com

Hancock Fabrics

National sewing and fabric retailer.

3406 West Main Street

Tupelo, MS 38801

Tel: 877 322-7427

www.hancockfabrics.com

Jo-Ann Stores, Inc.

National sewing and craft supplies retailer.

5555 Darrow Road

Hudson, OH 44236

Tel: 888 739-4120

www.joann.com

Michaels

National sewing and craft supplies retailer.

8000 Bent Branch Drive

Irving, TX 75063

Tel: 800 642-4235

www.Michaels.com

Sew For Less / American Sewing Machine

Online retailer of sewing and craft supplies.

516 First Capitol Drive

St. Charles, MO 63301

Tel: 866 739-2568

www.sewforless.com

Specialty Retailers

Got Buttons

Online catalog of buttons.

18121 E. Hampden Ave

Unit C, PMB#109

Aurora, CO 80013

Tel: 303 736-2920

www.gotbuttons.com

International Cutlery

Offers a full range of sewing scissors and shears.

367 Madison Avenue

New York, NY 10017

Tel: 866 487-6164

www.internationalcutlery.com

M&J Trimming

Extensive online catalog of buttons and trims.

1000 Avenue of the Americas

New York, NY 10018

Tel: 800 967-8746

www.mjtrim.com

Tender Buttons

Enormous in-store selections of antique and vintage buttons.

946 N. Rush Street

Chicago, IL 60611

Tel: 312 337-7033

143 East 62nd Street

New York, NY 10021

Tel: 212 758-7004

Thimbles Etc.

Fine quality sewing tools and accessories.

P.O. Box 745186

Arvada, CO 80006-5186

Tel: 888 844-6257

www.thimblesetc.com

Organizations

American Sewing Guild

National Headquarters

9660 Hillcroft

Suite 516

Houston, TX 77096

Tel: 713 729-3000

www.asg.org

Home Sewing Association

PO Box 1312

Monroeville, PA 15146

Tel: 412 372-5950

www.sewing.org

Clarice Taylor is passionate about needle arts and handcrafts. Working in humanitarian affairs she has, during her assignments, seized opportunities to experience and learn about sewing arts from all over the world. She has visited women's weaving collectives in Thailand and basketmakers in Uganda, Haiti, Rwanda and Tanzania. Among her favorite possessions is a hand-crocheted table cover from Bosnia.

Clarice started basic sewing in her Barbie-doll days. Standing 5'10" as a teenager, she found the skill useful in relieving herself of pant legs and shirt sleeves that were too short, and then began to add her own sense of design. Today, she employs her gifts for herself and her family. Her creations include 18th-century costumes and couture-style gowns for her daughter's theatrical roles. Her elegant, beautifully fitting cashmere coats often lead to requests from friends and strangers. She also uses her sewing and design skills in home décor. Using beautiful designer fabrics as well as unusual textiles from her travels, she has made slipcovers, pillows, duvet covers and curtains.

Her plans for the future include a home décor Web site, urbanvillagedecor.com.

Clarice believes in the intrinsic cultural value of needle crafts, that they are among the human endeavors worth preserving from one generation to another. ***A stitch in time...*** is her first small gift to that preservation effort.